I didn't know that

whales can sing

© Aladdin Books Ltd 1998
Produced by
Aladdin Books Ltd
28 Percy Street
London W1P 0LD

First published in the United States in 1998 by
Copper Beech Books,
an imprint of
The Millbrook Press
2 Old New Milford Road
Brookfield, Connecticut 06804

Concept, editorial, and design by
David West Children's Books
Designer: Robert Perry
Illustrators: Darren Harvey, Robin Carter, and Steve Roberts –
Wildlife Art Agency Ltd., Jo Moore

Printed in Belgium

10 9 8 7 6 5 4 3

Library of Congress Cataloging-in-Publication Data
Petty, Kate.
Whales sing : and other amazing facts about sea mammals / by Kate Petty ;
illustrated by Darren Harvey and Jo Moore.
p. cm. — (I didn't know that—)
Includes index.
Summary: Examines the many facets of whales and dolphins, including physical
characteristics, breathing, hunting, migration, and reproduction.
ISBN 0-7613-0738-9 (trade hc) — ISBN 0-7613-0819-9 (lib bdg)
1. Whales—Juvenile literature. 2. Dolphins—Juvenile literature.
[1. Whales. 2. Dolphins.] I. Harvey, Darren, ill.
II. Moore, Jo, ill. III. Title. IV. Series.
QL737.C4P49 1998   98-6804
599.5—dc21   CIP AC

I didn't know that
whales

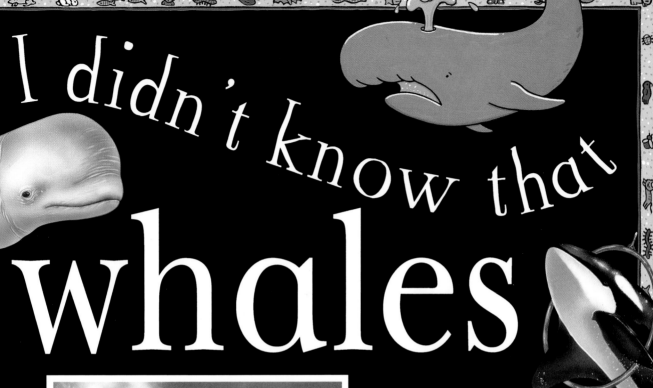

can
sing

Kate Petty

COPPER BEECH BOOKS
BROOKFIELD, CONNECTICUT

I didn't know that

Introduction

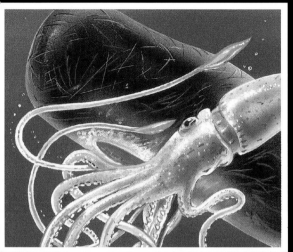

Did *you* know that whales are mammals that breathe air? ... that some whales are heavier than the largest dinosaurs? ... that dolphins help each other when they are sick?

Discover for yourself amazing facts about whales and dolphins – what they eat, how loud the humpback whale's call can be, how they have babies, who their worst enemies are, and more.

Watch for this symbol that means there is a fun project for you to try.

Is it true or is it false? Watch for this symbol and try to answer the question before reading on for the answer.

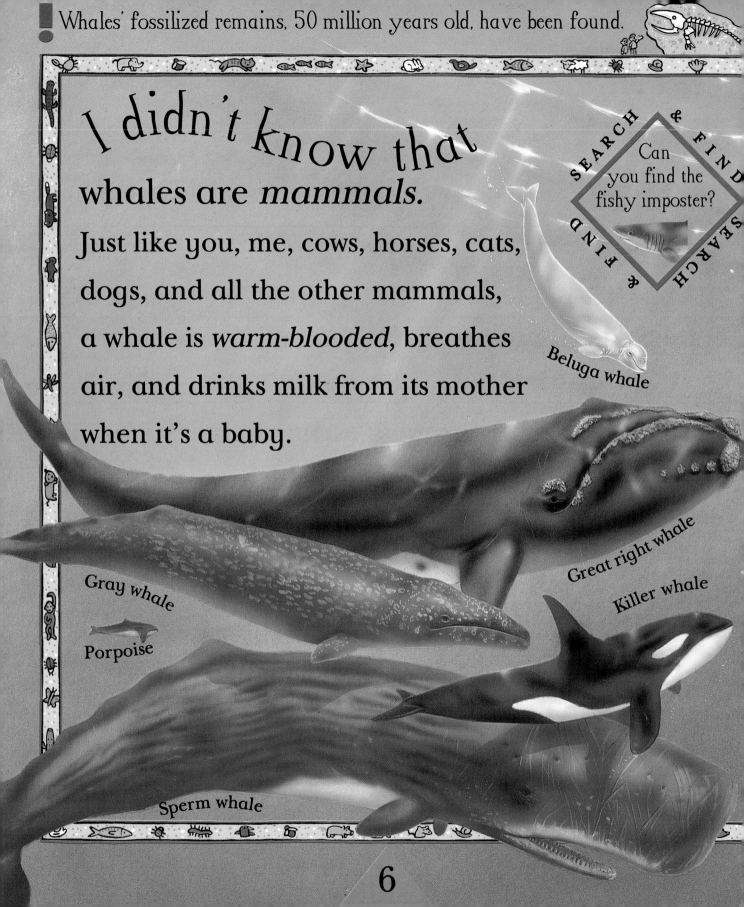

I didn't know that

whales are *mammals*.

Just like you, me, cows, horses, cats, dogs, and all the other mammals, a whale is *warm-blooded*, breathes air, and drinks milk from its mother when it's a baby.

SEARCH & FIND

Can you find the fishy imposter?

FIND & SEARCH

Beluga whale

Great right whale

Killer whale

Gray whale

Porpoise

Sperm whale

Amazon river dolphin

Narwhal

Bottlenose dolphin

Blue whale

Humpback whale

Whales don't need fur to keep them warm. A thick layer of *blubber* keeps them warm in the cold seas.

Vestigial limb

From being a land mammal, a whale's body has adapted to a sea-going life. Its front legs became flippers and its back legs disappeared altogether. If you look at its skeleton you can just see the remains (vestiges) of them.

Inuits eat whale blubber to protect them from the cold.

A blue whale's heart is four times the size of a man.

The blue whale is sometimes known as a sulfur-bottomed whale. On deep dives it picks up tiny algae that stick to it, making it glow in the dark.

Answer: **True**
At least! It weighs 900 lbs. An average man weighs about 220 lbs.

Blue whale

SEARCH & FIND
FIND & SEARCH

Can you find the penguin?

I didn't know that

a whale is the largest animal ever to live on Earth. The blue whale is four times the size of the largest dinosaur and 25 times the size of a large elephant. An animal this big couldn't live on land – but in the sea the water can support its enormous weight.

Brachiosaurus

African elephant

The tongue of a blue whale is the same weight as a hippopotamus!

I didn't know that
whales can hold their breath.
They have to! Although they are mammals that have *lungs* and breathe air, most whales spend a lot of time underwater. They come to the surface to breathe.

Blowhole

Lung

The *blowhole* on top of a whale's head is its nostril. The whale blows out air in a high spout before taking deep breaths and going under again.

Gray whale

A whale's lungs would be crushed by its weight on land.

Sperm whales were killed for spermaceti. It made good candle wax.

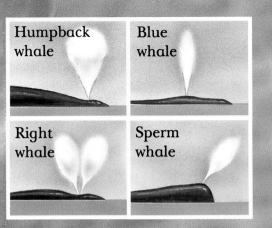

Humpback whale

Blue whale

Right whale

Sperm whale

True or false?
You can tell a whale by its spout, or blow.

Answer: **True**

A whale's spout is a cloud of vapor, made when the whale's warm, moist breath hits the cooler air. The pictures show spouts from different whales. Nineteenth-century whale-hunters would spot the spouts from a distance and could often tell from them what sort of whales were nearby.

Sperm whales hold the whale record for diving with dives of 9,000 ft, sometimes lasting over an hour. Their heads contain a waxy substance called spermaceti, which might help them to survive the *pressure* at such great depths.

Humpback whale

I didn't know that

whales are acrobats. Like this 50-foot humpback, many whales leap out of the water as they surface. They sometimes twist or somersault before crashing back into the water. This is called *breaching*.

Dolphin

Fish

Fish waggle their tails from side to side to move forward. A whale has strong muscles to move its tail up and down. It uses its flippers for stability and steering.

True or false?
Dolphins leap out of the water to frighten the fish.

Answer: **True**
Imagine the commotion caused in the water by a breaching whale or dolphin! The frightened fish crowd together into tight groups, which makes it easier for the dolphins to catch them.

Dolphins, including killer whales (the largest dolphins), perform in marine parks. People are fascinated by their agility and intelligence. It's sad that the dolphins are captive but the audiences learn that they should be protected in the wild.

An individual whale can be identified by the shape of its tail.

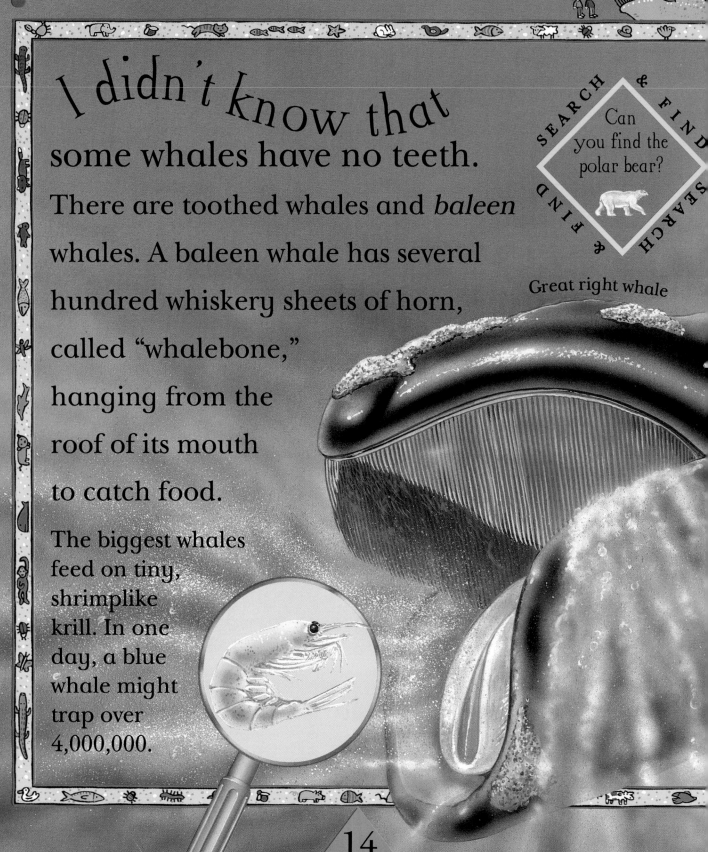

I didn't know that

some whales have no teeth. There are toothed whales and *baleen* whales. A baleen whale has several hundred whiskery sheets of horn, called "whalebone," hanging from the roof of its mouth to catch food.

The biggest whales feed on tiny, shrimplike krill. In one day, a blue whale might trap over 4,000,000.

SEARCH & FIND
Can you find the polar bear?

Great right whale

14

True or false?

Whales catch food with bubbles.

Answer: **True**

A whale can round up a shoal of krill by blowing bubbles as it spirals up from below them. The krill are spun into the center of the ring of bubbles where the whale can snap them up in one mouthful.

The whalebone corsets worn by fashionable Edwardian women were reinforced with strips of whalebone (baleen). Today, plastic would be used instead – but corsets have gone out of fashion!

Baleen whales may have evolved from insect-eating mammals.

I didn't know that

killer whales hunt in packs.
Killer whales, or Orcas, are
large black-and-white dolphins.
They live in groups called *pods*
and hunt together. They eat fish, squid,
seabirds, seals, and even
other dolphins and whales.

Killer whale

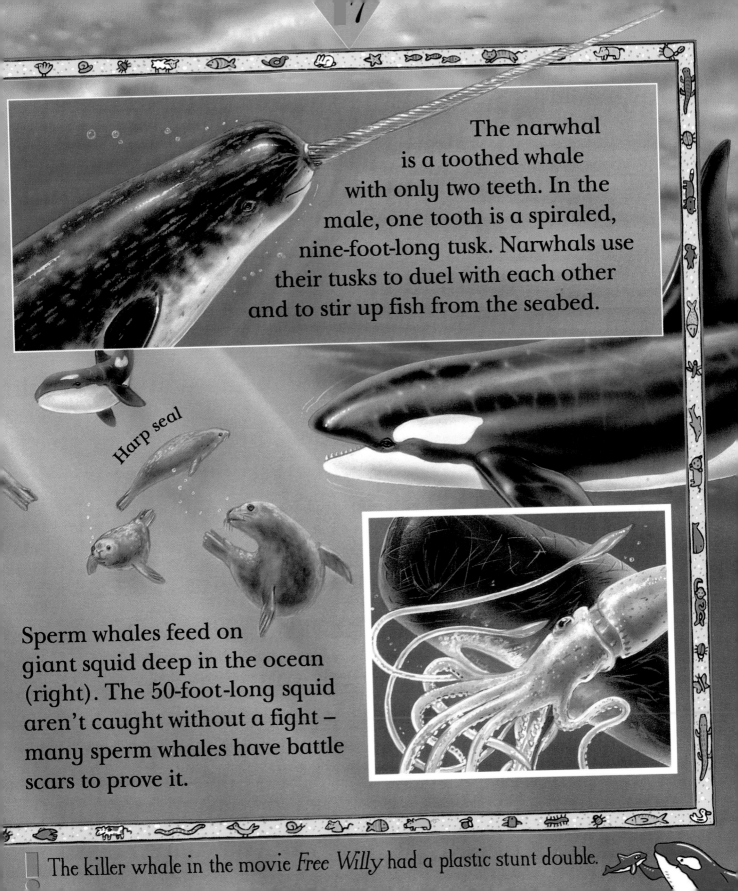

The narwhal is a toothed whale with only two teeth. In the male, one tooth is a spiraled, nine-foot-long tusk. Narwhals use their tusks to duel with each other and to stir up fish from the seabed.

Harp seal

Sperm whales feed on giant squid deep in the ocean (right). The 50-foot-long squid aren't caught without a fight – many sperm whales have battle scars to prove it.

The killer whale in the movie *Free Willy* had a plastic stunt double.

 **True or false?**
Whales are found only in the sea.

Answer: **False**
Dolphins are small toothed whales, and five species of them live in the rivers of South America, India, Pakistan, and China. Some Amazon river dolphins (left) live 2,000 miles away from the sea.

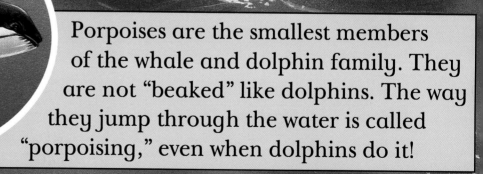

Porpoises are the smallest members of the whale and dolphin family. They are not "beaked" like dolphins. The way they jump through the water is called "porpoising," even when dolphins do it!

Dolphins will help an injured animal reach the surface to breathe.

Can you find the breaching whale?

I didn't know that

there can be thousands of dolphins in one *school*. Common dolphins gather in huge groups where there are plenty of fish to eat. Sometimes 2,000 of them will work together to herd and feed on shoals of fish.

The U.S. Navy uses dolphin intelligence! The one below is trained to locate and pick up torpedoes from the seabed. Others detect submarines and guard harbor gates.

Common dolphin

Migrating gray whales shower in waterfalls to wash off barnacles.

Gray whale

I didn't know that

some whales travel over 12,000 miles a year. Californian gray whales swim over 6,000 miles from Alaska to Mexico every winter to breed. They swim back for the summer when food is plentiful.

SEARCH & FIND
Can you find the killer whale fin?
FIND & SEARCH

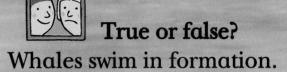 **True or false?**
Whales swim in formation.

Answer: **True**
Lots of whales, particularly dolphins, swim
in formation. Herds of belugas migrate
in formation as they file through the
pack ice. From above you can see
the formation (left) as they follow
their food south.

Whales can become stranded
if a beach slopes suddenly and
they are left without enough
water to support them. Their
friends swim to their aid and
then they too become stranded.

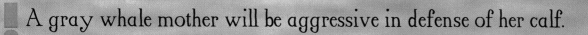
A gray whale mother will be aggressive in defense of her calf.

I didn't know that

whales can sing, communicating across many miles of sea. Each one has a distinctive and recognizable song. The songs are made up of rumbles, clicks, and whistles. They are noisiest during the breeding season.

Arctic sailors used to call belugas "sea canaries" (above) because of the loud whistles and bell-like calls they made.

Humpback whales are famous for their songs. Each year they have a new sequence of notes. They will play around with the sounds of this sequence for hours on end.

The humpback's song can be heard 100 miles away!

The humpback whale's song can be as loud as a plane taking off.

Humpback whale

Sound waves from dolphin

Echo from fish

Hunting dolphins use *echolocation*. They make a noise and wait for the sound waves to bounce back. Sound waves work like water waves. To see how they work, put a small cup in a sink of water with a dripping faucet. Waves from the drip bounce off the cup.

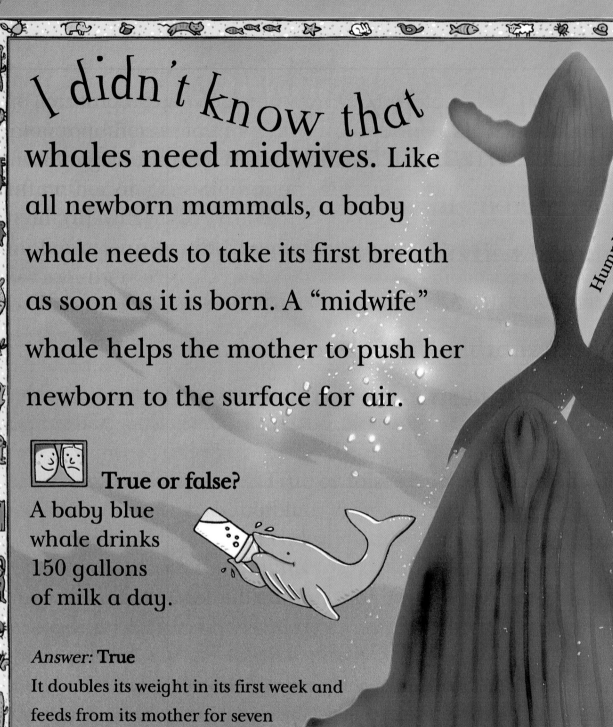

I didn't know that

whales need midwives. Like all newborn mammals, a baby whale needs to take its first breath as soon as it is born. A "midwife" whale helps the mother to push her newborn to the surface for air.

Humpback whale

True or false?

A baby blue whale drinks 150 gallons of milk a day.

Answer: **True**
It doubles its weight in its first week and feeds from its mother for seven months, until it is 50 ft long.

When they are courting, whales often play together. The male swims alongside the female, cuffing her or stroking her tenderly with his head. Humpbacks leap out of the water together when they are mating.

Male dolphins show off to females (below) with high-speed chases and fights. They bite and snap at each other, but they hardly ever die from their wounds.

Male right whales perform a courtship dance.

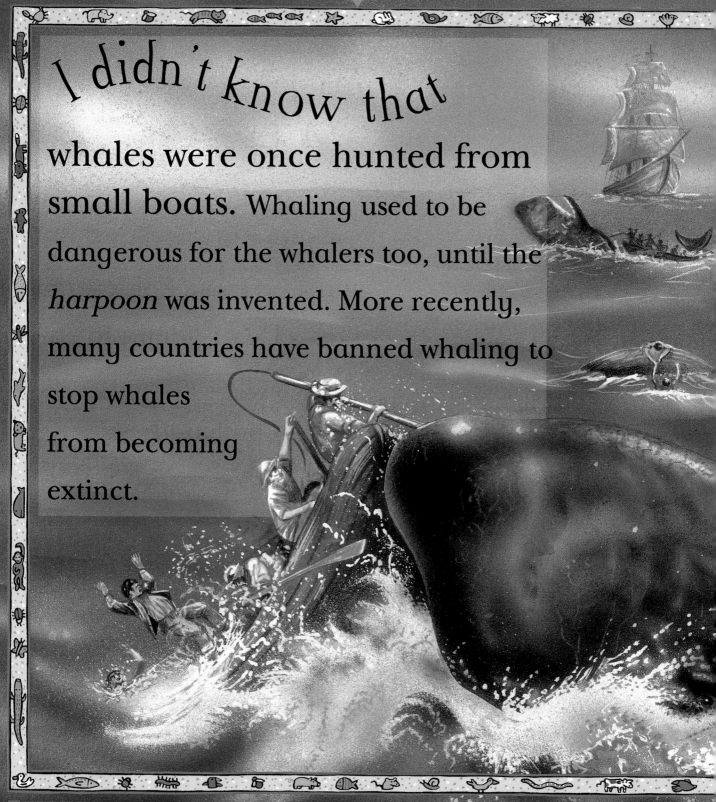

I didn't know that

whales were once hunted from small boats. Whaling used to be dangerous for the whalers too, until the *harpoon* was invented. More recently, many countries have banned whaling to stop whales from becoming extinct.

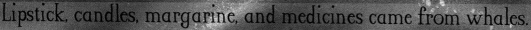
Lipstick, candles, margarine, and medicines came from whales.

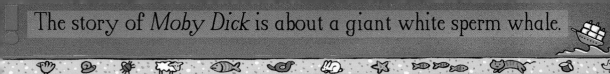

Factory ships have made it possible to kill whales and process their meat while still at sea. The whales are harpooned from catcher boats and their carcasses hauled into the factory ship for butchering.

Sailors used to while away their time at sea by carving pictures on pieces of tusk or whalebone (baleen). The carved pieces were known as scrimshaw (above).

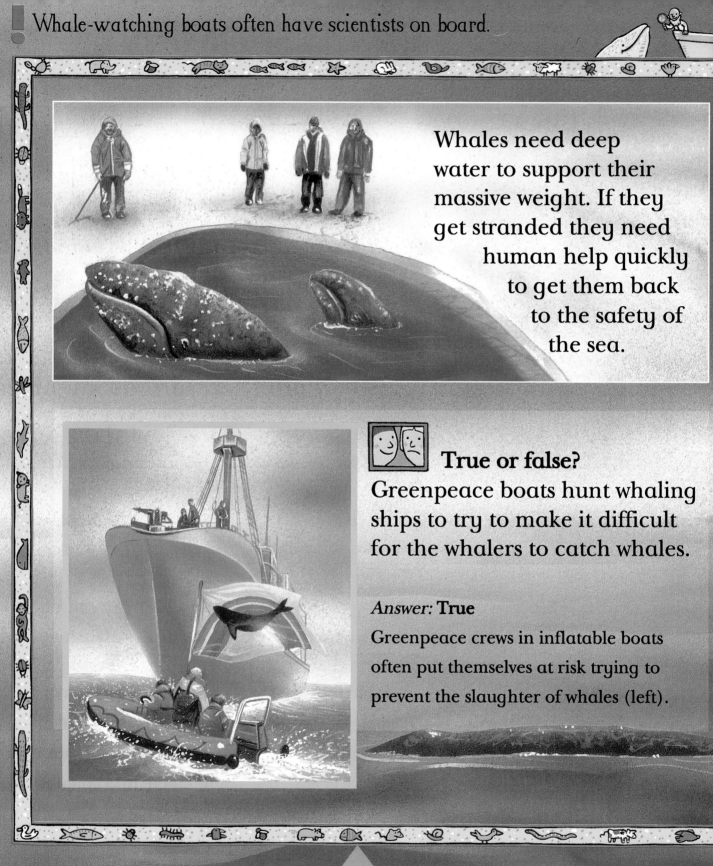

Whales need deep water to support their massive weight. If they get stranded they need human help quickly to get them back to the safety of the sea.

True or false?
Greenpeace boats hunt whaling ships to try to make it difficult for the whalers to catch whales.

Answer: **True**
Greenpeace crews in inflatable boats often put themselves at risk trying to prevent the slaughter of whales (left).

I didn't know that

you can go on vacation with whales.
Some travel companies take *"eco-tourists"* on
trips to see animals in their natural habitat.
Eco-tourism makes it worthwhile for local
people to protect the animals
rather than hunt them.

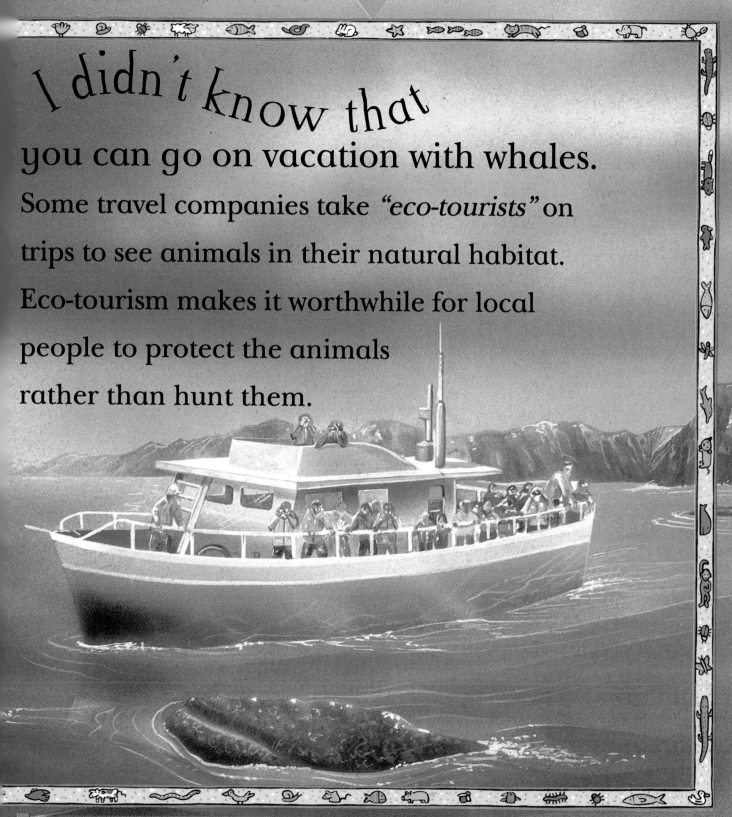

Whale-watchers must be careful around mothers and their calves.

Glossary

Baleen
"Baleen" whales are toothless whales. Baleen is the name given to the horny plates that hang down from the roof of a toothless whale's mouth to filter its food.

Blowhole
The whale's nostril on top of its head.

Blubber
The thick layer of fat that lies under a whale's skin and keeps out the cold.

Breaching
Breaking clear of the surface of the water.

Echo-location
Some animals use hearing as well as sight to find out where objects are. They make a sound and listen for its echo bouncing off objects.

"Eco-tourists"
People who go on vacation to see wild animals in their natural habitat because they want them to be protected.

Habitat
The natural place in which an animal lives.

Harpoon
A spike attached to a long

cord and fired from a gun, used for killing whales. It was invented in the 1890s.

Lungs

The organ in an air-breathing animal where oxygen is passed into the bloodstream.

Mammals

The group of animals that includes cats, cows, monkeys, etc. They are warm-blooded, give birth to live young, and feed them milk.

Migrate

To make journeys in search of food or warmth.

Pod

A small group of animals, especially whales or seals.

Pressure

The weight of water at great depths presses down on creatures not suited to it and crushes them.

School

The name for a large group of sea animals.

Warm-blooded

Warm-blooded creatures make warmth inside their bodies. Cold-blooded creatures are warm or cold according to the temperature outside.

Index

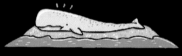